ROI

Return on Investment

A SYSTEM. AN INVESTMENT. AN UNCERTAIN OUTCOME.

E. L. Blackstone

Printed in the United States of America

ISBN 979-8-9975168-0-2 (paperback)

ISBN 979-8-9975168-1-9 (ebook)

Published by 21st Century Better Products & Services (21BPS)

Denver, Colorado

First Edition

JANA

Disclaimer

ROI: Return on Investment reflects E. L. Blackstone's personal experiences, observations and perspectives from more than two decades within the federal prison system.

This book is provided for educational and informational purposes only and does not constitute legal advice. Federal policies, procedures and individual circumstances vary and may change over time. Readers should consult qualified legal counsel and appropriate official sources regarding their individual circumstances.

Author's Note

21 years inside the Federal prison system.

The Federal government invested hundreds of thousands of dollars in my incarceration. Housing. Food. Security. Transportation. Medical care. Administration. Year after year, money was spent to keep me confined.

From a business perspective, that raised a question for me: **What is the return on that investment?**

I watched men enter the system and leave differently. Some developed, some were consumed, some went home prepared, others left more damaged than when they entered.

The system can shape you, strip you, teach you, harden you, or break you. Somewhere inside all of that is still the question of what you choose to do with your time.

I wrote *ROI* to share what 21 years taught me about navigating that environment, understanding its dynamics, and preparing for what comes after it, if that is truly possible.

For someone preparing to enter federal custody, I want you to understand things I had to learn through experience.

For someone already inside, I want you to recognize that your time still has value.

And for everyone else, I want this book to raise a larger question about incarceration itself:

When we invest this much in confining a human being, what should we expect the return to be?

Introduction: Was it Fear or Lack of Fear?

I often look back and wonder why I didn't snitch. Was it fear or lack of fear? I could argue lack of fear because I always thought I was clever enough to think myself out of situations I couldn't fight my way out of. Maybe it was fear, because I am and always have been deathly afraid of how I'm perceived by those I care about. Whatever my undertaking, I need to be the best that I can be. Basketball player, Janitor, Rapper, Entrepreneur, or Drug dealer.

A healthy fear of the right things can be a life saver, just as an unhealthy fear can be a show stopper. My reputation is everything to me, and I have guarded it with my life, and my twenty-plus years in federal prison is my most stubborn example. How smart could I be, if I managed to end up in prison, let alone for that long? Opinions vary, and a person's perspective will determine whether I or anyone else who has encountered this fate was, in fact, smart, stupid, unlucky, or some sort of victim.

The Federal Government, The Department of Justice, those US Attorneys and their assistants have about a 97% conviction rate. Any person or entity with such a gaudy record would always be primed and ready for a confrontation. And so they are. This system of ambitious and highly motivated people go about their business with ferocious efficiency and achieve results that can awe the most slippery of magicians.

But I am not going to bash federal prosecutors—I have the utmost respect for anyone and any organization that is the absolute best at what they do. Plus, as I said before, they are people who can't seem to lose, and whether what they do is personal or business for them, they nor the system they navigate are perfect. I am a forty-something who has been incarcerated since I was a twenty-something, for transgressions of the law that a jury of my peers determined I was guilty of during both of my jury trials. I won't cry and whine and ask the community, "Why me?" I won't complain of being doubly oppressed and handicapped by what many have correctly described according to their experience as systemic injustice.

Now at the end of my sentence for my crimes, with one year or less left inside the prison, I'm going to see how well-prepared I am for life after prison. The Department of Justice invested $30,000 a year for twenty-plus years in my incarceration and rehabilitation. With my return to the free world inevitable and imminent, we'll all experience together my successes and failures.

But soon, we'll also all be able to judge whether the Goliath that is the federal government is indeed the same titan of tangible returns when it invests in its citizens such lofty amounts of resources as twenty-plus years of incarceration demand by the return on investment on E.L. Blackstone.

Chapter 1

Infected with a Sense of Hope

Being in the courtroom had started to feel normal. The old, magnificently crafted rooms had started to lose their majesty. The cold place where people came to be charged by a human, convicted by humans, and then sentenced by another human was no longer grand and intimidating.

My mother and various family members were on non-verbal speaking terms with the clerk. You could almost feel the empathy from the stenographer and the courtroom officer, as they had surely seen countless families enter prayerfully and exit in shock and disbelief at the outcome of the proceedings.

I was very fortunate to come and go from the courtroom with my family, dressed in clothes from home, fed with food from a nearby restaurant, sometimes even after performing normal Dad duties such as dropping kids off at school. No jumpsuit, handcuffs, or shackles for me, no rough housing by a zealous U.S. Marshal, no sitting in the bullpen in the basement of the courthouse. I didn't experience that until the guilty verdict in the second trial. When the judge entered, we would all rise just like on TV, and he would insist we all sit down. I had been there enough times, it felt like he was a decent guy—as if manners and etiquette were eased with him, like when there is a family gathering as opposed to a formal one.

This ease and comfort, while relaxing and pleasant at the time, proved dangerous. My entire family was infected with a sense of hope, and with only a 3% chance of victory, we didn't have a snowball's chance in hell of leaving every court session as a complete unit. So finally, after numerous court appearances, the gut-wrenching and back-breaking process came to an end.

On April 30th, 1997, I emptied my pockets, told my mother and my girl I loved them. My attorney headed for the exit just as he said he would. I was cuffed and led away, and as I headed toward the prisoner elevator, I cussed myself for ever wondering what it looked like back there. When I was tossed into the holding cell with the rest of the chattel, I looked like a guy in a tuxedo at an office party, my autumnal-colored shirt and pants the only non-prison-issue outfit in sight.

There was a short van ride. I don't mean it was actually quick—the process of moving eight prisoners from one location to another is a detailed and exhaustingly long ordeal—but when you are on your way to prison, it seems like you pull up to the building in no time. Then I was processed into the Detention Center, which is the federal equivalent of the County Jail. Guys are housed pending court or transfer to prisons, some transfer to County Jails for other charges, and some are actually awaiting release. Once you're inside the labyrinth, there is a light-headed, hazy feeling that comes over you—at least, it came over me.

It was a foreign land, strangers everywhere, and nothing

was quite right. I longed for the familiar feeling I had developed at the courthouse, not just because it was outside of the lock up, but because we all desire comfort in our present situations. So I wished for the intake to be over so I could find a bed and sleep until I could figure out a way to cope. I wasn't hungry, I didn't want to replace the smell of freedom with the smell of jailhouse soap, and I didn't want to talk.

After negotiating the maze of doors, the last door stood in front of me. I had my bed roll in my hand, my ill-fitting jumpsuit covered me, and the guard asked if I was ready, as if I could actually declare that I wasn't ready and he would personally offer some reprieve reserved for only the special prisoners. That door opened, and I didn't know what to expect.

When I stepped inside the pod, I smelled a decent food odor. It was so pleasant, in fact, that I remembered it was now six p.m. and I hadn't eaten since that morning and I was, actually, hungry. The door closed behind me, and I had my marching orders:

"Get a tray out of the hot box, then report to Room 15. We lock down in two-and-a-half hours, so if you have questions or problems, see the officer in his station."

As I finished the horrible food that wasn't as bad as I feared, I began to scan the day room.

There is a certain awareness that must be kept in prison environment. For too many reasons to name, you need a visual on as many people as possible as quickly as possible, and unless you feel like a gorilla, as discreetly as possible.

Race is King. So no matter my crime, my look, my demeanor, the Blacks had to be the first to approach me, and conversely if I was a social butterfly, I would go to the first Black person or group of Blacks to begin my orientation. This is true for all races. People are weeded out by crimes, sentences, and whether or not they cooperated with the authorities, and sometimes, more or less sternly, depending upon the ever-changing culture of the temporary holding facility.

There are always exceptions to rules. Even in this preview to prison, there are reasons for the races to mix, but pay attention, there MUST be a reason. If a Black guy doesn't associate with other Blacks and his crime is drug dealing because most drug dealers in the Feds are Black, then there is a reason—that reason could be because he is a snitch or other complications.

If a White guy doesn't rotate with the other Whites and, for example, his crime is Child Molestation—because most child molesters in the Feds are white—his crime is the lowest of the low and it's punishable in many ways. So these individuals often come together as a way of protecting each other simply by not being alone. Having someone to eat with, walk the track with, play cards or chess with means the world to a person in this predicament.

The reasons for races mixing isn't always inherently bad, but there is always a reason. I can recall about two months into my six-month stay at the Detention Center, I was introduced to an older hustler and pimp. He was sort of a legend where I'm from. I didn't know him, but I'd heard of him. He liked me, he liked that I was solid, and he expressed sadness at my twenty-five-year sentence.

Oddly, there were only two reactions from people learning my sentence was that length: one, they would gravitate toward me, or two, they would just look at me without advancing or retreating. Some thought I was a damn fool for not cooperating for a lesser sentence, and some wouldn't even try to imagine being in my position.

The important thing to keep in mind is that I am not

special. Not unique. Not better than anyone else who has gone through this. No one is. The two bank robbers I befriended, both in their forties, one took the deal for twenty-seven years. WOW, he took a deal for more time than I fought for! His co-defendant took the case to trial and got life—whoa, he wasn't fighting a good fight!

So back to the Big Homie. He was older and smoother than most people in the lock up. He had less stress, too. He was just in on a violation—he would be in prison only one-and-a-half years.

I noticed he had started holding conversations with a middle-aged white guy. Like hours at a time, daily, for almost a week. Then one day, Big Homie came to me and told me, the guy was a white collar guy who was just waiting for a bail hearing and then he would be gone.

But when the guy was pulled over in his Porsche and taken into custody, he was allowed to lock his car and have his family come and get it. The issue was, the area where the car was sat right on the border of a neighborhood where you didn't see this kind of car. Sure enough, his family had been hesitant to go to the area at night, and when they did go to get it the next day, it was gone, and it hadn't been towed.

So here's the play: the Big Homie told the white guy I was a gang leader, that the neighborhood was my turf, and I would probably know who had his car and could get it back, and now, he was bringing me in on the scam.

My part was easy. Look mean and say very little in the presence of the soon-to-be victim. Then when this poor guy was thoroughly convinced I could get his car back, all I had to do was go to the phone, call my girl, and spit some gibberish on the line about some of my homies taking a car and having to put it back or else.

The guy listened to my words. My girl was confused, but she just listened to my rant. I later explained it to her on a face-to-face visit. Big Homie brokered the deal; the favor was worth $1,000. Two days later, the guy's car was found, the usual stolen car damage done—broken window and ignition but otherwise unharmed.

I was told to fill out a commissary list for $100, and when the appreciative guy brought the bags to my cell door, I stayed in character, and he left.

Chapter 2

Turning 26

A few weeks later, Big Homie was sent to the prison for his violation, $900 richer on account of his scam. He pimped us both, but who could complain. The guy got back a car he thought he might otherwise not get back, I got some commissary, and Big Homie got enough money to cushion his eighteen-month stay. There is always a reason for racial mingling in prison.

Just to put it all in perspective, I had only been off the streets for days when some of these lessons and realities became apparent to me. I promise you, I was lucky!

My original sentencing date was my birthday. That isn't the kind of thing you're allowed to cry about and point to as cruel or unusual punishment. Nobody involved in the process gave a damn if August 21st was my birthday. If a day didn't fall on a weekend or a federal holiday, it was business as usual.

However, during a scheduled call to my attorney in which he was oblivious to the upcoming date's significance to me, I was able to half-heartedly joke that perhaps me being sentenced on the day I turned twenty-six years old could be an omen of something good to come.

My attorney, who was excellent at his craft, once told me he knew he was impressive, as the private investigator happily and adamantly attested, and that if we were to lose, it had nothing to do with the validity of our case and certainly not his effectiveness as counsel. It would simply be because federal juries are not constructed to acquit. Then, in terms he felt would strike a more personal chord, he explained,

"You are these people's worst nightmare, your appearance is menacing, you're charged with drugs, and those white people will not let you go free."

He also asked me what I thought were my chances of beating the case.

I thought it was a silly question—either you win or you lose, so it was 50/50.

After he finished a very rare laugh, he corrected me: he said 20%.

The entire time we prepared for trial, he tried to talk me out of going to trial because he would need five chances to put it all together and secure the elusive win for the defense in a Federal Criminal Trial.

Clearly, I didn't listen.

However, I have no issue with his performance. There was a point in the first trial in which we had a chance to ask for a mistrial, and the judge talked us out of it, all but saying the words, "Based on the evidence and testimony in the case, there is no way a jury will convict"

With all that behind us, and it being brought to my attorney's attention that sentencing was on my birthday, he had the court date moved, and I finished the summer and fall in the Detention Center, and because it was all I knew, that was fine with me. I was thirty minutes from home, and I was acclimated. I felt like I could do my entire twenty-five years right there—only being able to go outside every other day for two hours was acceptable, and I had to adjust.

So on sentencing day, I woke up that morning so hopeful. I just knew God had a miracle in store for me. My smart ass wrote this dynamic statement to read to the judge to persuade him to see the error in his sentencing me at all, let alone for twenty-five years. My family and friends had all written letters of character reference and pleas for leniency, and I don't know how they misrepresent this shit so absolutely on television, but the prosecutor referred to my loved one's words to the judge on my behalf as proof that I was some sort of dangerous character with far-reaching influence and thus, I needed the most time for the crime possible. I was really upset by that. Whose parents wouldn't write on their behalf? Whose siblings wouldn't? How their letters turned us into a crime syndicate escapes me to this day.

During my soliloquy, I made some points about how I didn't think the jury was qualified to judge me, and some other points I thought showed I was thoughtful and witty. The judge was slightly impressed, and the prosecutor very irritated!

I suppose a dumber person would have been received as more humble, and my attempt at sounding intellectual was taken as arrogance. I can say this now because as I look back, the prosecutor reminded the judge with no respect for his position or his opinion that if he attempted to sentence me to anything under the least amount of time she recommended, then she would see to it that his sentence and order were overturned.

It was only like ten seconds, but it seemed like ten

minutes as I observed the bitch-slapping the Assistant United States Attorney put on the Federal Judge. I observed a truth common citizens only learn when they are in a court at a sentencing hearing: the Prosecutor is in charge, not the Judge.

I'll repeat it using different words: the Judge can do anything in the courtroom he wishes *except* go against a Prosecutor who has invoked a statutory sentence.

So all that shit the Judge said about me being intelligent, and eloquent, and my having a point about the harsh sentence, and how locking me away was a waste of potential, was just that—shit. What the Prosecutor said was law.

After admitting his hands were tied and that I would be going to prison for twenty-five years, he was nice enough to recommend I be housed close to home, and that is a big deal...until it becomes common knowledge that a Judicial Recommendation holds no weight.

So he slammed the gavel and ordered me remanded until my sentence was completed. My family and one of my friends were there, and I wondered how they felt. Not how they acted because everyone was stoic and silent, but how does it feel to see your loved one sentenced for a non-violent crime receive more time than some murderers and rapists?

When you consider yourself someone's partner or protector, these are the very outcomes you feel like you're supposed to guard against, and not only are you saddened by the fact of a twenty-five-year sentence, you are made numb by what you perceive as your failure. That is how my parents described it to me on one of our visits. My mother once told me she felt like she was locked up with me doing day for day.

That sentiment made me want to die. The way my mother felt made my oldest sister feel as if our mother lost her willingness and ability to love her children other than me.

Both those women passed away during my prison sentence. Am I wrong for the relief I feel because my mother and my sister are no longer suffering those particular emotions? You would be astounded to learn all of the attitudes and tweaks in personal philosophy required to navigate a prison term to completion and remain sane.

Then there is the ever-present doubt that you actually remained sane. It has been said that going to prison is such an unnatural act, it's supposed to make you crazy, and if it doesn't, then you were already crazy when you got there.

In taking all of this into consideration, I could easily come to the conclusion that I already was, or was going to go, crazy. And by standing by me, my family and friends were going to go crazy, too, or they would have to let me go in order to save themselves.

Either way, my family seemed doomed—the Feds, the Dope Game—I had ruined my family, my community, or tested them and stressed them to the point they'd never be the same again.

We won't know if that's good or bad until I'm released and the people of the United States of America discover their ROI.

Now it was time to take the training wheels off.

I told you I was lucky, so when I was finally on the bus to the Big House, I couldn't complain when we stopped at the prison around the corner literally from the Detention Center as they both sat nestled in the foothills a mere half-hour drive from my home. After all, the ride to the southern end of the state where I would be housed was only a two-hour drive.

About an hour into the drive, we pulled up to what, to

me, looked like an empty movie lot—the lot where they filmed *Con Air*—only this was no movie. When the bus I was on pulled into the Air Field, there was an assembly of buses, and after all the buses arrived, we all sat in silence, cuffed and shackled individually on the cold vehicles while the guards went about their business lightly, joking and conversing about a range of topics you can't help but hear in the silence of the carriage.

Then the Air Lift arrived, and things got serious quickly.

Suddenly, there were guards everywhere, sunglasses, bulletproof vests, and shotguns all around, and the transfer process began, with people exchanging buses, and from the plane to the buses, and from the buses to the plane.

This is where I really got to see the assortment of people housed in federal custody all across the country.

Guys with hair so long and matted, you suppose they have been in a dungeon for twenty years and they might be enjoying the excursion, the fresh air, the scenery. New people and walking a straight line as opposed to the circles they must travel in their little cells. Guys with tattoos that cover their heads and faces, guys made huge by the years of lifting weights, along with the skinny, pale guys who must surely be the victims of the horror stories you hear about in prison.

Here, you will see a few women, as well, the lost and the lonely women who suffer even greater fates than the men because female prisons are few and far between compared to the men's facilities. The women who could be librarians, the women who were undoubtedly drug addicts, and those who might be in prison because of someone else in their lives.

And as all the prisoners were shuffled, the buses loaded

and the plane secured and ready for takeoff, the guards calmed down again. As the plane lifted off, the guns and paperwork and sometimes property were all stowed under the buses again, and one by one, the buses left, headed for their final destinations.

Once on the road again, I was back to my dreamlike state. The fresh stimuli had caused me to be alert and aware —after all, to be aware is to be alive, and with a twenty-five-year sentence, I couldn't get enough practice living! The lazy, quiet drive was hypnotizing, and I calmed down whether I wanted to or not. And another hour later, we arrived at the Federal Correction Complex.

It didn't look like a group of gladiator pits. None of the four institutions looked like a slaughterhouse, but I guess you don't find much blood at the front door of any butcher shop, either.

Chapter 3

The Hole

We arrived at about four p.m., and that is a National Count time—if you're in prison at that time, you're in, but if you're not, you aren't, and nothing moves until the count is right at every prison in that complex.

So we didn't make it off the bus until about six p.m. From the road, I could see guys playing basketball, bocce, baseball, and jogging, and various other exercises.

Just seeing this lightened my mood, and I hoped to get inside the fence only to get to the yard before it got too late or too cold that early November day. Everyone who arrived at the facility I was designated to was promptly escorted to the SHU—or special housing unit, otherwise known as The Hole, which is where you are segregated from the rest of the prison population.

We were placed in surprisingly roomy cells by twos. The cell had a shower, bunk beds, a desk, and the combo sink and toilet but with enough room to do push-ups or even burpees. I was shocked. But with such large accommodations, I feared this was a long-term set up.

However, this was a cooling off tactic. The Captain at this prison preferred all new arrivals to sit in The Hole for a week, to adjust their attitude to suit him and his staff.

After your week in semi-isolation, you get to meet with the Captain and his special crew, the SIS Unit, responsible for the security of the place. To no one's surprise, the Captain was an extremely abrasive fellow, with a familiar face and build. Being a sports fan, I recognized that he looked just like a pro basketball player, but that recognition was of no use here. He wouldn't be impressed by my knowledge of the game and awareness of his brother, so I didn't comment.

This screening was all about irritation and agitation and it was easy to fail, and failure earned another week inside The Hole. Just think, this what I got just for being designated to this place. This might be a good time to start whining and crying about the conditions. After all, I didn't even ask to come to this place.

But I decided I should wait before I began filling the suggestion box with helpful ideas on how to improve their initiation and orientation. Good idea to wait, too, because the Captain was more concerned with making me tell him what gang I was affiliated with and refusing to accept that I had no known enemies to be receptive to any new guy issues I might have.

Apparently, according to them, every group in prison constitutes a gang. Every gathering of three or more people not directed by or okayed by staff can be broken up—Bible, Koran, Torah, or Football in hand—at an officer's discretion. All the officers work for, and are a representation of, Mr. Attitude Adjuster himself, the Captain.

I barely made it, but I did. I passed the screening, and I was ordered to laundry for my clothes.

Being sent to the Housing Unit where I would sleep was almost a joy because of how difficult it seemed to be to get there. I toted a mesh bag full of ill-fitting clothes, shirts too small, boxers too big, khaki outfits old and worn, towels seeming colored and used. Later, I would understand all this is by design so the laundry workers can sell you items that are in good condition and actually fit.

Given my cell assignment, I took my things into a four-man cell made for two men and put my stuff away, made my bunk, and stepped outside to begin my bid.

As I walked around the unit, I noticed a certain chatter, some legal mumble-jumble about an issued that could shorten some drug sentences.

This is how I would do my time, I thought.

I would embrace all sensible and reasonable theories, methods, pathways, and hopes for a much shorter sentence than the twenty-five years that currently hung around my neck like an invisible but all too real noose.

I'd heard the chatter back in the Detention Center, but I was still too new to the process to know I should be excited. The Congressionally-appointed Sentencing Commission, whose job was to keep federal sentences fair, effective, and reflective of the wants and needs of society, had voted and had determined the sentences for crack cocaine at the ratio of 100:1 compared to powder cocaine was unfair and unusually harsh, and they had recommended Congress eliminate the ratio and the disparity.

Because this action had gained momentum and buzz worthy of a terrific ad campaign, the couple of years it took to actually be submitted to Congress had flown by, and the guys were talking. After all, Congress always adopted the recommendation of their commission.

So just as I was set to get used to being in prison for the

time it would take for my appeals to free me, it looked like there might be some legislation that would be even better than the legal fight I was taking to the juggernaut inside the Prosecutor's Office. Only four or five years before, there'd been crack riots in the federal system, the result of the first failure, or refusal, depending upon your point of view, to modify the statutes that were filling prisons at the rapid pace to beyond capacity.

But Congress, for the first time since the creation of the Sentencing Commission, did not adopt or enact their recommendation—there would be no shorter sentences.

I has been hopeful for the change in law, and I was disappointed. I was like a sport coach who was prepared to have his team play but would gladly accept a victory due to forfeiture or other technicality. But I wasn't totally crushed, because I had all my appeals right intact and in action.

I began getting to know the place, the nuances, the rules, and the culture. I was firmly established in my "car" which is a group of prison associates bound together by color/race/experience/geography/affiliation/or habits and activities. This is also the group that is as much like a gang to the officers and prison security as the Republicans and Democrats are to the wayward youth who learn from politicians of all the different methods of division and conflict from ideology, to tradition, to color—Republicans being white and Democrats all darker shades, or in another analogy, Republicans being red and Democrats being blue. Just like street gangs because there is nothing new under the sun.

I started playing sports which was extremely dangerous in prison because health care is carried at a bare minimum. You can imagine a medical school's best and brightest aren't pining to be contracted in a prison. I was also taking any classes I thought would keep me sharp as I waited to be liberated. Although most classes were offered to prisoners closer to release, in order to prepare them for life after prison. I understood this logic enough, and that with twenty-plus years to do, I was at the end of every list.

I found comfort in the reality that most of the classes were bullshit taught by the prisoners because of their knowledge in basic math or social sciences. Sadly, the era of prisoners obtaining real college degrees in prison was over, and I would spend my entire prison sentence trying to piece together a degree from the occasional pilot program that various community colleges would offer at various prisons around the country. I would find solace in the books I read and the sports I played along with the classes I took—these things kept me sane through almost every negative occurrence during my prison term.

When my direct appeal was denied, I stayed positive, never believing I would do more than twenty years in prison. I saddled up for the next appeal; I played basketball and watched football and took classes and tried to be the picture of strength and composure to my family and friends.

As I was getting used to being in prison, the people I cared for outside of prison also began to get used to me being in prison. Other than my parents, I wondered and worried constantly who would not be in my life as the days passed. Letters slowed. Contributions to commissary slowed. Interest waned. Those who were my best supporters needed to move on and have lives.

Chapter 4

The Appeal

God is good, though, and I was blessed during every minute of my incarceration to have someone interested in my well-being. One door shuts; another opens. I remember when my pregnant girlfriend told me I would need to accept her new baby in order to keep her and my children in my life. In my lifetime, I have seen and known this ultimatum to work. After all, no one is an angel, and there is usually room for everyone to forgive in order to move on.

But me being two years into a twenty-five-year sentence, there was no reason for me to cave to that demand. If she'd had another baby in two years by someone she wouldn't name, then I didn't expect to see my children too much more, and possibly not know them by the time I got out if I didn't win an appeal.

So my relationship with my daughters was now in jeopardy just as my relationship with my son was prior to me being locked up. Life is rough, but it's fair—I'm the one who went to prison, so I couldn't expect any of these people to do the time with me. Poor Mom.

So I followed the jailhouse advice of one of the Big Homies—to stay open because I never knew who would be there in the end. He was right. I'll say again, I was blessed because I would receive just enough interest and attention to distract me from how fucked up my life actually was.

My writ to the Supreme Court was denied. So I no longer had an attorney. Now my 2255 Appeal to the judge was up to me. No more classes. Just my appeal and sports until I wrote this appeal, but wait, with all these blessings and distractions, and time flying, I had earned a transfer to a lesser security facility.

It was a great thing that I still had support and someone to talk to because it would be overwhelming to go back through the transit. Con-air was unsettling as ever, except I'd be boarding that dilapidated plane as part of my reward for never being caught breaking the rules, I would be sent over a thousand miles from home to a friendlier prison.

Just before I was put in transit, I finished my self-written 2255 Appeal. I prayed over it and walked it to the mailbox, and I started the latest wait.

With my mind clear, I had signed up for a class, and when I was notified of the transfer, I used the vocational class and the pending appeal to try to postpone the move. I spoke to my case manager and my unit manager because I was pretty sure it was written somewhere that you're not supposed to interrupt appeals. Yep, written in the seldom-read section of the policy statement that governs the running of the institution, and the first of what would be a total of five transfers in twenty years proceeded. A fourteen-day ordeal, three different hold-over facilities, and my first real insight to dealing with a person who had cooperated with the law.

My guys at the first place were tight and right. No

snitches, no homosexuals or child molesters allowed. We all read each other's paperwork and could vouch for one another. My Big Homie from the neighborhood was so thorough about weeding out the weirdos, I never had to until I transferred. I noticed the guy they had me shackled next to for parts of the trip would disappear for other parts. He was a snitch and his co-defendants were in the system, so whenever we came to a place where he might encounter one of them, they would put him in protective custody or more correctly, The Hole in that facility until our bus left again. It was unfortunate because he could have been useful. He was from the state where I was being sent, and he was an alright guy except for the glaring character flaw that made his trip more eventful than mine.

Upon arrival at this place, we were taken straight to the laundry for our clothing and bed issue, then sent to our housing units. I was mistakenly put in a smoking unit, and the next two weeks was hell until I was moved to a non-smoking unit. I had more than a couple intense discussions and issued a couple of invitations to a quiet place to wrestle about my neighbor's habit of blowing cigarette smoke in my direction as I slept. I would wake up daily feeling the emphysema settling in my chest. I still don't know how many days were taken off my life. I had to have smoked second-hand two-and-a-half packs a day for those two weeks.

But besides that, my stay there started off well. I had a couple of visitors from home come see me, and the effort people make to come see you is a big deal, and it tells people the kind of person you are and the kind of people in your life. Big Homie who ran the scam on the guy with the Porsche told me to pay attention to the mail call, as well, and be leery about a guy who never got mail. For sure, if their mother doesn't send at least a birthday and Christmas card, this guy is a piece of shit who likely burned everyone in his life.

So with plenty of mail and a couple different visitors, those who paid attention would have considered me a good guy from that alone. The new place also had a couple of professors from the Community College come in so I was determined to get that education, after all. When my appeal came through, I could use the classes as more proof that prison was indeed wasting my potential.

However, the release date was still an issue. Luckily for me, the professors were serious and cared about the students, but the officers weren't and didn't, and they operated on a first come first serve basis, and as long as the $10 per class registration fee was on your books, they didn't care.

So with the same zeal I would later use to gain control over a TV and also be written up for, I would attack the lines for registration early and often, and I am proud to say that I didn't miss any classes, even though some were redundant. I took them all and maintained a 3.8 grade point average. My only grade under a B came when I was dealing with the reality of less contact with my kids and their new families.

It was just sad that I had to lie, omit, trick, and aggressively apply myself to take these classes because by the time I would have been eligible by release date, the classes would no longer be offered or I would no longer be at that facility. I sort of had to maintain those undesirable criminal and deceitful ways in order to put myself in a position to possibly somewhat begin to point my compass in a direction of positivity. So for two years straight, I focused on my classes from this small college. I was proud of myself, and those who were standing with me waiting on my appeal were proud, too.

What bothered me was that my oldest sister was taking classes at the same time and she would tell me about the cost of the classes, and when I told her they were only charging us $10, she cried. She said it wasn't fair that prisoners could be educated so cheaply when she was struggling to pay tuition. Yep, me and my sister fell out, and I quickly invited her to trade places with me.

So while I waited for my relationship with my sister to return to normal because I loved her dearly, another unexpected detractor made herself apparent.

I had a unit manager who seemed to be impossible to please and accused me of being lazy and not participating in programs and said I may be on the road back to the other prison that is unfriendly but closer to home, which would be a dilemma. And I was offended because I had become a model prisoner through my educational efforts.

It turns out that the college classes weren't automatically keyed into the system like the classes the prisoners and prison staff teach. So she was unaware I was in school at all. I was allowed to exit the meeting to get my transcripts, and when I returned to show her, she could not doubt me or question my intelligence or my work ethic and desire to better myself.

However, she did not have to give props, either, and she did not. That was fair as long as I wasn't penalized for failing to take the knowledge I was acquiring as the goldmine it was and keep it moving. Within the next year, she would be implicated in a sex scandal with a married coworker and she would lose her job for a drunk driving incident that required her to wear an ankle monitor.

Meanwhile, I was super anxious about my appeal. I was

told the lengthy time for the decision was a good thing because they usually denied appeals rather quickly. But the anxiety was infectious. My parents, who had joined a prisoner advocacy group and were coordinators for our state, had used their connections to get the lawyer for that organization to look into my appeal—to check the status or push it along by making the inquiry.

The lawyer's phone call brought the sky six feet from the top of my head. She said the judge never received the Appeal. I had been waiting for over two years for an answer that would never come.

Chapter 5

A Much-Needed Boost

In my ignorance of the law and my rush to remedy the problem, I took an extra copy of my appeal and mailed it right off to the judge.

In record time, like four weeks later, it was denied, and he explained in the denial that it was too late for appeal. They allow you one year to submit it, and I had done so in less than three months, but he'd only received the second copy almost two years after the time limit had expired.

I was not crushed, though. He said in the denial if I could prove the original appeal wasn't late or offer a good reason it was late, he would rule on my reasoning and might allow the late appeal.

Piece of cake: I had my return receipt from the original mailing.

I would prove they transferred me wrongfully after I informed the BOP of my pending Appeal, and if nothing else, I found case law that allowed that the post office could have lost it, and if I would forgive the post office, the Court could, too, and we'd move on with the process.

Here is when I got crushed. The return receipt was

nowhere to be found. It had been in a folder that contained a copy of my PSR which is a tell-all about a guy on his case, and these are used to discover rats, so the BOP stopped allowing us access to them, and my entire folder was confiscated. With no proof I mailed it, all I could do was insist the Post Office had lost it and agree I wouldn't hold it against them.

Denied.

Do you have any idea how hard it is to pretend you still have hope in your case, faith in the system, and a positive outlook to people who look in your eyes daily, and people who look for your letters and calls for insight on how you're managing? Poor Louise, still doing day for day with me, and these days were getting harder.

At that point, I fell into stereotypical prison time. I played sports, lifted weights, watched TV, and talked a bunch of frivolous shit! I counted all the celebrities' money, I memorized all the video girls, and I saw every show and game available on cable. I turned in my schoolbooks and occasional biography and self-help literature for fiction, action heroes, and urban books, suspense thrillers by authors who are mainstays in every prison library and book cart. I used the various men's magazines for current events and sources for conversation with any pen pals.

I started officially spreading false hope about my release date. I always managed to say, "I'm waiting on a response from the court" or "My attorney has something going," but the truth was, the fear or lack of fear conundrum had me refusing to say that my appeals were exhausted and I was simply doing time. I felt like saying that would cause my loved ones to believe I would give up and then go too far to keep me from doing so, and the fact was, I didn't want to talk about it. I needed to rest.

Holding up the banner of hope was an all-out effort, and I was at the end of my strength. The time and distance did what time and distance do to relationships—strain them —and I lost contact with long-time friends and romantic interests while trying desperately not to seem desperate to hold on to others.

I got a much-needed boost. My parents drove sixteen hours with my kids to see me. It is hard to pack five years of love into four seven-hour visits. I was blessed to have parents who would gather up the crew, drive in, and trust I had established a decent enough set of ties to that community that someone at the end of the drive could watch and entertain my kids while my parents who were an older couple could rest and recuperate after the drive.

I sent my parents a picture of my friend so they would know his name and face. If I trusted him, then my kids and my parents could trust him, too.

But only in the lives of people affected by a lengthy federal sentence would Grammy and Papa ever meet a recently released convict whose crime was drugs but his profession was pimp in a parking lot and turn over control to all their heirs and then sleep for hours with no way of securing the situation. I'm blessed that there are good people everywhere and to have learned: *Judge not lest ye be judged.*

I was energized from the visit with my family, motivated to improve my active relationships, inspired to keep hope alive, and I continued to have faith that the greatest Legal System on Earth would eventually allow another chance at freedom. Time flies when you do not give in to the notion that you're doing it or that you'll do a lot of it. I was busy, reading and writing and being who my friends and family expected me to be. They would reach out to me to hear something positive, and it turns out the ability to be positive is a magnet, and an aphrodisiac.

Months riding this new energy, and then one of my best friends and at one time a serious girlfriend called the prison to inject pain, confusion, and the fear of God into my life, all in the name of being a good friend.

She called to leave a message to call either her or my mother because my mother was in the hospital and the diagnosis was cancer.

I waited the requisite hour until the next opportunity for movement on the prison compound and went to the phone room to get to the bottom of this. You've heard "don't shoot the messenger"—well, I would suggest avoid being the messenger because the bearer of bad news is forever associated with the bad news; it's human nature!

I reached the phone, called my mother's cell phone, and true to form, between her and my Pops, they had smuggled her phone into her hospital room and they awaited my call. She knew I would need to hear her voice. I am Momma's boy number one, and Momma was right!!

Lesson to all those people who think their parents are old and square and incapable of being slick and cunning. My parents had arranged for my mother to see me for the last time under the guise and with the added pleasantry of me seeing my children. This is why Papa was exhausted from driving and Grammy handed the kids over to a pimp in a motel parking lot. This visit HAD to occur, and nothing would prevent it, and in true forsaking all others fashion only, Mr. & Mrs. Eugene. Blackstone knew their complete and total mission. But those two kept up their clever deceit as they maintained she was in a good place, doing well the entire (less than a year) cancer fight, they would tag-team me, telling me how well she was doing, keeping me hopeful and positive.

It worked—I handled her illness well. I last spoke to her on a Wednesday. We laughed, and she promised she was stronger every day. But when I called on Saturday, I called specifically to corner my Pops. I knew Louise slept late these days, exhausted from her radiation treatment, so I called early before basketball. On Saturday mornings after they closed the chow hall, the gym would open, so we would have from seven a.m. to nine a.m. to play some good basketball, after which I would shower, then after count, I would go to lunch and sleep the afternoon away. This was my schedule pretty much until I got too old to effectively play hoops out there on those courts.

So I placed my fifteen-minute call at about six-thirty a.m., but when my sister answered the phone, I instantly knew something was wrong. The time zone I was in was an hour ahead of the time back home, so the second I heard her voice, my equilibrium was off. I lost my balance and dropped to the floor with the phone to my ear. I landed with an actual thud—I heard it because the phone room was empty at the time. At the time of her acceptance of the call, I was numb and dumb. I literally couldn't comprehend. I held my breath until my body was forced to breathe.

Chapter 6

His Tough Ass Cried

The volume in my ears went in and out. I heard her say, "She is gone, El" and I asked who was gone, and I don't remember what she said immediately after that.

But I needed clarity, so I asked her who had left and where she went. After all, my mother might have been at an early doctor's appointment or she could have been out of the house walking, enjoying the fresh air. Or she could have been on a plane or in a car on her way to see me on a surprise visit. After all, my Pops didn't answer the phone, either.

It could have been, right?

No.

I don't know what my sister said after that, and I don't know when she gave my Pops the phone, but his voice brought me back from the delusion I had entered. He was describing her last moment, her last breath. He had held her in his arms, and watched his wife and the mother of his children take her last painful breath. He completed his vows and honored them with a dignity that is so rare, it seems mythical.

As I listened to my father calmly explain to me the circle of life and how Louise had entered a new phase, I heard his pain, and then he confessed it was time and it was best because "she was as weak as a kitten."

They had lied all the way to the end to spare me the pain of being away and helpless as our family lost our matriarch.

I couldn't hurt at that moment—I had to let him hurt.

So we sat in silence until the fifteen-minute call ended. Then I got up, checked to see if I had money on the phone system for another call later, then I headed to the gym. That's what I had to do. I must have been hooping, too, because I don't recall sitting to watch because sitting would have led to thinking and I didn't think about shit.

I also didn't hear shit—the counselor and the chaplain kept calling for me on the loud speaker. I couldn't hear it, but between games, guys would come and tell me. I blew it off, without telling them what I was going through. I would just shrug my shoulders and holler "Ball up!" to start the next game. That morning, I was following instructions: when I was little and I was going through something, to keep me from crashing, my mother would send me to the basketball court.

At age ten, at nine p.m., I would be instructed to go shoot baskets for a little while at a nearby park, so when I needed to loosen up or stop thinking, I would play ball on my mother's orders.

After my shower, and count, and lunch, I would deal with the passing of Mrs. Louise Blackstone. The BOP has Policy and Procedures for allowing a prisoner to have bedside visits, or attendance of a funeral.

Over the course of the next few days, my father and I would talk more than we talked on the phone in all the years I had been locked up, in the effort to postpone the funeral while I jumped through hoops to get there.

In a nutshell, I would have had to pay for two officers' airfare, a rental car, and overtime for the day, along with my own expenses, in order to attend my mother's services. When my case manager informed me of the cost and told me to come back once I had the financials arranged, he did so thinking I wouldn't be able to afford it, or I couldn't afford it in time.

So the next day, I came in and explained that we needed to make a phone call. I had a friend who needed to know where and how to send the money. He was flabbergasted and frustrated. He was supposed to have done some paperwork, gather signatures, to run some logistics. He had not done that, and he had to inform me his supervisors probably wouldn't sign off on it, even after he'd sent me on the hunt for money. I wonder, did he feel bad for misleading me that way?

No complaints, he was doing his job to the best of his ability. I could see the fear in his eyes when he broke the news to me that his boss would be the problem. I likely said a silent prayer that I wouldn't act the way he thought I was capable, and in his mind, he figured out how to summon help quickly should this meeting go south.

So I let my Pops know I wouldn't be able to come, and he was deflated. He had used some of his nervous energy on my endeavor and really wanted a positive outcome.

This would be the second funeral I'd now missed. With such lessons of loss, with so many permanent situations, I can say to you that the punishment portion of my sentence was hitting home, and it wasn't taking twenty-five years.

They poured plenty of pain into my prison stay. Are they thinking about the ROI?

With there always being something going on in the federal system, we were informed that the institution was adding another building that would house four units, thus increasing the population of the prison by 25%, and we could opt to stay in the older units or move to the newer one.

This is the sort of thing no one can anticipate and which disrupts the entire balance of a prison. Some embrace the change, others loathe it—this was the equivalent of being transferred. The landscape of the prison changed, the makeup of the units changed, and more and more new people would come in a rush, so the prison beds could be filled because everyone in prison knows the BOP hates empty prison beds—they are bad for the budget.

I looked for anything to take my mind off the loss of my mother and the strained relationships I now hesitated to nurse due to the growing disinterest of people not in prison. Looking into the sky meant thinking of the future which meant missing my life and wishing all my days away. It is vital for your health and security to live in the moment, to feel the pulse of the prison yard, to know the tensions and pay heed to the warning signs of danger.

Allowing the culture of the prison to absorb me was a good way to stop thinking. I simply let my newly developed instincts take over. You have to assume there are no good people and act accordingly—they call this [11]Bidding: becoming immersed in prison life is Bidding.

So as I got back to being a stereotypical prisoner, too

much TV and not enough contact with my increasingly shattered world outside of prison, there was something going on in the courts, and Congress again.

The tape was thick and bright red as always, but there was some movement in the mindset of people who mattered, and that Sentencing Commission was at it again. They hadn't quit as I feared; they hadn't been on vacation and been getting paid not to work, as I figured.

They had been gathering information, and they maintained that the 100:1 ratio was unfair. But this time, they were prepared to act autonomously in an effort to draw attention to and correct the disparity that existed in federal sentencing.

Our sources, our reason, our experience all told us not to put too much stock in the rumors about potential change. Even the most jaded of us couldn't help but imagine if it was true. As the momentum gathered strength, the more guys wanted to know, the two-and-a-half years of build-up flew by, and we anxiously awaited a vote.

Then it came down. My celly and I were in the TV room when we saw the bottom line on CNN: "Federal Sentencing Commission votes to reduce sentencing for Crack Cocaine, retroactively."

Stunned, we sat and waited for it to run again, and when we deduced we both couldn't have imagined the identical phrase twice, there were no words. I was ten years into my twenty-five-year sentence; my celly was fourteen years into his twenty.

His tough ass cried, a silent two-tear cry, and then he left the TV room and headed down the rows in the unit to inform the other guys who might be affected.

Mind you, the Crack Law was basically a Black Law, as only a few whites or other minorities were involved with and incarcerated for Crack Cocaine. So that made this another racially tinged issue. Nevertheless, the Blacks were buzzing. Soon, letters began coming in from various lawyers and public defenders about the new law and how to go about researching to see if and what kind of reduction all involved could receive.

Talk about energized!

I was back enrolled in a relatively new class, a Personal Training course with a real license and certification from a company on the streets. I wanted to be prepared. I wanted a marketable skill that the prison, the Probation Department, the prosecutor, the judge, and society at large would all recognize and hopefully accept. Trying to be smart, to show that I could educate myself in general without a specific field to apply it to, had proven personally gratifying but unimpressive to the powers that be thus far, and I would not leave this opportunity to chance. I was determined to show I was ready!

Chapter 7

How Long Does it Take?

Late that year in November, the reductions started being revealed. In the spring, guys would begin benefitting, and in December, I received my certification as a Personal Trainer. I was ready! Indeed, I was ready.

By February, I learned that my celly would be leaving in the summer, and I also learned that I would not benefit from the sentence reduction. I would still be required to serve 87% of my sentence, which would have me incarcerated until 2019.

I heard from my court-appointed attorney who explained to me that the only reductions will be for Guideline Sentences and sentences above the mandatory minimum for that crime. Because the prosecutor in my case charged me with a Statutory Sentence rather than a Guideline Sentence, which promised the same sentence length, my sentence could only be lowered by an act of Congress or me turning into a snitch, not lowered by the Sentencing Commission.

Total Fucking Bummer. Talk about some Bullshit!

Over two years, my family had been just as sure as I was that I would be home sooner, and as always, the hard part was explaining to them what I didn't fully comprehend. Worse was telling my friends and companions that the plans we made were no good, that their loyalty and support would not be rewarded at this time. The effort they voluntarily put into my cause may be wasted energy because my lawyer won't even submit a motion on my behalf citing an assurance that I'll be denied. But wishing me the best should I decide to file a motion on my own.

So if for nothing else, I had to research the law, dust off my typewriter ribbon, and submit a new motion for those who stood by me, hoping and praying for my relief.

Two months later—denied. No complaints, this is life; I'll just pretend to be happy for those who got some time off. I would hold my smile as a guy who was now leaving would come by my cubicle to leave me a pair of gently used sweats, or a sports watch he wouldn't be caught dead wearing outside of prison, as gifts along with the reassurance that my day will come, they would continue to let us out.

And just as I was prepared to concede that I was, in fact, cursed, another potential blessing came my way, to detract me from my latest denial: I was being considered for a minimum security prison.

All I had to do was complete a Gate Program at this facility, which was a work assignment outside the prison gate, to see if I was trustworthy. This trip to the minimum security prison could lead to an unescorted bus ride, it could lead back to my home state, and it could lead to a place with no fences and no need for knives and gang culture.

So I signed up for the Gate Pass, went back to watching sports, and put my focus on getting closer to home. My children were teenagers, my Pops was having an issue with his leg, and my oldest sister was having liver problems. I needed to take advantage of the chance to get in closer proximity to them.

Fuck that sentence reduction, the law, the lawyer, and everybody who got time off. It didn't profit me, so to hell with the entire situation.

Now getting through this phase wasn't complex—I just had to hand over the keys to my car and stop my daily habits of prison participation, but it wasn't easy, either. There are always things happening, fires to put out, truces to maintain, fights to have or referee. Just like people have to be careful and mindful of others going through rough patches like death and denials that can lead to hyper-violent situations, there remains an element of here and now that always must be dealt with and respected, and guys don't care about your issues, plans, or goals before their own.

So as I changed my patterns to work and then workout and TV only, I had to learn to enjoy the inactivity and how to make the days pass at this new slower pace. My guys respected it for the most part, and soon, the car ran as if I had never been a part of it, except the occasional call to advise on an internal beef. I was now gone. This was perfect as I made efforts to reconnect with family and friends who thought I would be happy I was coming closer to home or with a certain friend with would be ecstatic if I were to transfer closer to her location.

I couldn't lose as long as I was at a minimum security place, and I handled the days cautiously, avoiding potential altercations by wearing a happy face and laid-back demeanor. Six months on the gate pass and I would be free from fences. I was dropped off at a gas station by two officers, handed my itinerary, and told to wait there for a shuttle to the airport.

Being outside of the fence for the first time made me dizzy. As I stood in the parking lot and looked up to the sky, the combination of the blue sky, the sun, and trees was like a kaleidoscope. I had to sit on the curb to gain my balance. I had $25.00 and a bus ticket. I went in the gas station and made my first non-commissary purchase in over a decade. Soon after I'd enjoyed my iced tea, my Doritos, and my Blow Pop, the shuttle arrived, and I was on my way.

I was counting my blessings once again, and although I was heading to another prison for another decade, life was good. That's right, life was good. I was supposed to catch a light rail train from the airport to the bus station, but that shit might as well been from the Jetsons. I missed the next two trains because I didn't know how to catch them, and I realized I wasn't too excited about asking for help. All these strangers—I'd feel silly asking how to catch the train.

So I walked around until I found the platform and I watched until I observed what to do. Then I was off, feeling good except for the fact that my bus left in seventeen minutes and it was a twenty-minute ride on the light rail. Nevertheless, I was headed to a place with less stress and more freedom. I would see my dad and meet my grandson. Blessed!

I had a great trip. I was across the street from where I first began my sentence, but this time, I was able to see up and down the hills that hid all the prisons on the complex. I could see the highway that led to the complex, I could see my visitors as they arrived, I could walk to the parking lot. There were no fences that kept me from them, no metal detectors that kept them from me, and as luck would have it, the new President of the United States wasn't shying away from the effort to continue to work on sentence disparities, so there was plenty to talk about when I saw my family.

Without prison politics—well, without prison politics dominating the yard—I just moved about enjoying the close proximity to my loved ones. By car, they were only ninety minutes away.

Once I got my routine established, I was able to do Good Time. The buzz had returned about the sentencing reform, and the proposed changes would affect many more people than had gotten relief just three years prior. When the vote was scheduled, we had a TV in the rec area on CSPAN. We were amateur analysts using our experience and feelings to guide the votes in like screaming at your horse coming down the final stretch.

Unbelievably, the Act passed. We hooted and hollered and celebrated because it appeared as though our elected officials had begun to listen to their constituents or had gotten involved in the business of granting mercy. With both chambers on board, the new 18:1 ratio was sure to be signed by this President.

I read everything that came out about this new legislation because I was once bitten. I got a severe pain in my stomach the first time I read the words "...Did not indicate Retroactivity." If they don't say it, then no one will do it. Anyone already in prison could not have their sentence changed to reflect the new more lenient ratio of 18:1, so if you had not received a sentence reduction to this point, you would not be receiving one based on this new law.

But this time when the court-appointed lawyer refused to file a motion on my behalf, and I proceeded to do it for myself and the judge denied me once again, he did so with a statement in his decision that said he agreed with me, that he would let me out of my prison if he could, but once again, his hands were tied. That damn prosecutor who had long moved on to a new and more powerful position was still in the judge's chambers. Although it was a new judge, she bitch-slapped him just as she did the first one.

We appealed, hoping to set a circuit precedent. This time, the lawyer assisted, and as usual, we were denied. At least I was close to home, I could share my misery with family and friends and not the fellow prisoners—all those guys I wish I'd never met. My faith in the system was once again shaken, and as I smiled at this round of guys leaving, my sister had been threatening to apply for clemency on my behalf. But filing for clemency causes you to give up your right to fight. Asking for clemency was throwing yourself at the mercy of a court you'd never set foot in.

So when my Pops got sick and my biological father passed away, I had begun to give seeking mercy some serious thought. Before I could do so, or even tell her about my decision to follow her advice, my sister had a stroke, was put in a coma, and then passed away. She was supposed to come visit the weekend she had the stroke. She was never aware I would do what she said, but in her last big sister call, little brother had been listening.

How would I get over this hurdle?

Well, for starters, I was armed with case law that made it possible for me to attend my sister's funeral; I needed to be with my family because we were being decimated by life. I contacted the same lawyer who had helped me lose all my appeals, and I asked that he file for permission for me to go to the funeral from the court. He suggested I request the escorted trip again, since I was closer to home and at a minimum security facility, they may grant it.

I had no belief in the BOP or their ability to treat me as a living breathing person with feelings and/or emotions; clearly, that is not in their job description. The lawyer had never heard of the provision I uncovered that would allow me to attend. So we made a deal: if he would research the case law to see that I was correct, I would go through the escorted trip request process again, and if he did indeed find I was correct and my request was denied, he would file on my behalf.

I made the request on Monday, and on Wednesday, I was disrespected in a way that makes me cringe at the thought. My Unit Manager called me to her office to inform me that my request had been denied, but she neglected to actually read the request as she explained that the Warden and all the other Power Players would never agree because of the amount of time I had left on my sentence. She referred to my sister in the present tense as if she were alive, and she was denying my bedside visit. I stood in silence, and just before my head exploded, I told her my sister had passed away, and my counselor interrupted my next statement by asking me to step outside.

I watched through the glass as she was now reading my request. Then I was summoned back into the room so she could tell me the request was now denied because the funeral home was in a bad neighborhood.

I was tired of going numb. Was this how you really survived a prison bid—by not feeling?

How long does it take a mortal to lose all feeling inside?

Chapter 8

Caught with Contraband

I had paid attention over the years, and I was learning the tendencies, tricks, and tactics of BOP staff—I knew I could win this fight. So I emailed my attorney, and he put the denial of the request in our motion for an emergency interruption of sentence to attend a funeral.

But I still had to go through the steps of telling the majority of my family that although I was just over an hour away in a facility with no fence and the freedom to walk away if I chose to, I could not get approval.

I collaborated with my sister's daughter to fill in the blanks for the attorney as we worked secretly on gaining approval from a higher source.

On Thursday afternoon, I woke up from my nap—all this thinking was draining, all this feeling and emoting was like a weight I had to carry, and I just wanted to sleep. I logged on to my email account and saw a message from my attorney titled: "GRANTED!!"

My sister was dead, my Pops was sick, and I was going to look at my family cry and join them in mourning—share the bereavement.

Why was I so happy?

Was it because I had won? Was it because I would see all of my family? Was it because I would feel the freedom of loving hands and kind eyes on me in my time of need?

I still don't know why I was so happy. But the staff at the prison wasn't done trying me, or attempting to punish me beyond necessity.

Next step—the staff had to review their copy of the court order, determine it was real and it was right, then call me and officially inform me I could go so I could arrange a ride. I already knew from my attorney that I could leave at ten a.m. Friday due to return Sunday at four p.m.

I waited all day for them to call me. I knew the last staff left at nine p.m. At eight-forty-five p.m. Thursday night, I walked to the office I was just in days earlier being denied. I saw my counselor sitting with the court order on his desk with his hands on his head. I knocked on the door, and in a frustrated and surprised tone, said, "It's legit."

I asked him if he intended on calling me to tell me, and he indicated he would have called me before he left for the night. But clearly, he had been tasked by his bosses—the camp administrator and Unit Manager—to expose the order as a fraud or find a technical fault with it, but he could not.

Two years before, I had ridden a bus unescorted across the country, twenty-nine hours on a BOP-sanctioned furlough transfer, but now, they were afraid I would escape if they let me go see my sister off.

The next morning at ten a.m., I sat in the R&D with that officer refusing to process me out. She had been ordered not to until the administrator called her. Then her phone rang, and it was her boss's boss. I needed to be gone in fifteen minutes as the federal judge had ordered.

Maybe the judge wasn't the punk the prosecutor made

him look like. I planned to remember to write him a Thank You note once I returned to prison and got settled back in.

My ride was outside, and when I approached, my friend handed me her phone—my daughter would not hang up until she heard my voice.

There was no staff there to receive me back on Sunday, so I spent the night in the SHU. When I returned to the compound the next morning, I immediately went about the business of looking for more ways out of prison.

Those two-and-a-half days had made me thirsty again, but I still knew my feelings were different. I no longer just wanted the government to see the error of their ways and let me out. I had no thoughts of being rehabilitated and just needing a chance to show it. At this point, I felt like I had been cheated, lied on, set up to fail, and then punished because of my color and particularly for having the audacity to test the Criminal Justice System in hopes of acquittal and exoneration.

I was browsing a prison advocate's email, and I found what I was looking for. There was a case pointing out that it was specifically unfair to certain appellants that judges couldn't even consider their motions and appeals. This seemed to cut at the power prosecutors had over judges.

I researched it, sought input from like-minded guys, and filed a motion the prosecutor would oppose as usual, but my motion would be allowed to proceed. Then, my court-appointed attorney was put back on the case because I was in over my head. Clemency didn't matter, if I had a chance to win a fight, and it was no longer about right and wrong. I was just tired of being stepped on—I was fighting just to fight.

While I fought for the sake of fighting, I began to show I had lost respect for the entity. The institution was like never before, and the only reason I didn't crash and burn sooner is because of a recent positive force in my life and the three classes I took in an effort to kill time. I was in a small pilot class offered by a nearby community college, covering renewable energy. I also took a correspondence course to be a Drug Treatment Specialist (DTS), and I attended a short drug class the prison offered, so I could see how to run a drug class.

Amazingly, I completed every class and course, and the whole time, I enjoyed contraband, and took liberties on visits, and disrespected the authorities at every turn. I no longer did anything to please or appease them. I did what I wanted for my own personal designs. I no longer cared where I did time—I was feeling abused.

Then I was caught with contraband, and in the matter of three months, I would give up my minimum security status for another round of transit treatment and an institution with the all too familiar fence and sense of despair that accompanies it.

But my new case was proceeding nicely, and when I arrived at the new place, another sentence reduction had been proposed by the sentencing commission.

I wouldn't fall for that again. I concentrated on the fight I had knowing the prosecutor would scrap as if it was the freedom of that office at stake.

The new place was a culture shock. The population of the prison was the largest I had been in, and while I was away at the prison camp, the lower FCls had experienced a population shift. Sex offenders were now a large portion of these facilities, and for the first time, I saw them as an actual car or gang. Their numbers had exploded to the point that they no longer cowered at the sign of trouble, and when called out, they would support each other all the way to the offices in which they snitched about prison beefs.

They were now a force in prison—if you had a disagreement with a sex offender, or child molester more specifically, all they had to do was claim that you were harassing them because of their crimes. The same way snitches are a protected class, the person accused of bothering a sex offender is locked up in The Hole first, then they ask questions. So you either leave sex offenders alone, or kick ass mercilessly—there is no safe in between.

So for the first time in my BOP career, I began complaining. Homosexuality was rampant. I suppose there was an in-between. In this institution, many of the sex offenders were homosexual, and that allowed the closet homosexuals to express themselves. So to pass the time as quietly as I could with as little interaction with suspect guys, I took yet another course in Personal Training, followed by a prison-taught CDL class.

Times like these twenty-six months I was forced to be in this place made me miss my Pops. I needed advice from a man whom life had taught me was truly wiser than me and would always be. So I would sit and think about him the last time I saw him, sitting in a room in a Senior Care Home, wearing donated clothes, wheelchair-bound due to a leg amputation, suffering from dementia.

When I was allowed to attend my sister's funeral service, I visited my Pops, and when I walked in the room, he was sitting in the center of the room staring at a collage of pictures of his family. A big picture of my mother was the center piece; his children, grandchildren, and great-grandchildren bordered Louise in smaller pictures. He stared at it as a child might stare at a TV screen. I wondered if it was dementia or the longing to be with his wife, or be in the company of his offspring and their offspring.

I took my Pops to get a fudge-icicle and a piece of chicken that day, and that was the last day we talked. So I sat in my cell and relived that day as often as I could bear it, for perspective. I had problems with my surroundings I could overcome, but my Pops was stuck. So while I did all I could to kill time, learn another skill, and earn my way back to a minimum security, the damn Sentencing Commission struck again.

They passed another sentence reduction. This time, all drug sentences would be shortened, in an effort to ease overcrowding of nonviolent offenders and to quiet the rumblings that the current President and his Administration was only concerned with helping Blacks. I still resisted the news and the excitement that accompanied it, but it was too big.

I began to receive emails and letters about it. When I would make calls, people would tell me they saw on the news that all drug offenders would receive time off, and with seventeen years in, everyone just knew I would finally catch a break. Then to top it off, the President expanded his Clemency and Pardon criteria so more people would qualify.

This was too much.

Then the legal mail started to come. Without me making any inquiries or efforts to contact lawyers about any issue other than the one I was fighting in court, the lawyers were contacting me. All I had to do was agree to let them research my case and represent me.

I told my current lawyer the situation and solicited his advice. He said there would be no conflict, and he suggested I put all the irons in the fire. So I did.

Now with all this potential good news, I was flying

through my course, and I completed the entire program in six months when they would allow over two years. No sense in playing a game—if I could position myself for success, I should. If I was going to get out early, I would be ready, but the BOP had nothing to do with any of it. They would continue to punish, and punish well.

After a few months of all the excitement, guys started getting sentence reductions in the mail, but the reductions wouldn't go into effect until the next year. They decided that so many sentence changes would bog down the courts, so they gave the system a grace period. It was so serious, I had an 800-number that I had my concerned loved ones call, so they could hear when my new sentence would be revealed. I was caught up in the hope of it all. But my time for floating on air would be brief.

Chapter 9

The Cost of Jet Fuel

My appeal in court was denied. The judge was allowed by the Appellate Court to review my case, and when he did, it was the same situation—nothing had really changed. If he lessened my sentence, the prosecutor would appeal, and the Circuit Court would follow precedent and increase my sentence to the original. I didn't tell anyone. I decided to let them keep enjoying the prospect of Clemency or the all drugs minus two law.

I started doubting everything once again. Just had to stay strong and keep that upper lip stiff. I read about fifty pages of a book once—this book pointed out all the problems with positive thinking, hell of a thing. Was it time to finally abandon positivity? Does thinking positive sometimes prevent you from seeing a situation for what it is? Never mind leaving prison early, do I stand a chance of being successful by any measurement whenever I do get released?

The thing about being behind a fence is there are more guys with more time and more guys with the fighting spirit. I ran into an older guy when I arrived at this place. He was a jailhouse lawyer of sorts, and I presented a few guys I learned had long sentences with the case law I was using when I got there.

That's how it's done. If a case has the potential to help someone even if it's not you, you're supposed to share it. There are likely some children, parents, or spouses who would be most appreciative. The exceptions are child molesters and snitches—no reason to help those kind in my personal philosophy.

So as I was licking my wounds from another loss, the older guy, as reciprocity for the case I gave, showed me a case he had found. This case was aimed specifically at the prosecutor. This case involved a judge who asked a prosecutor to admit that a prison sentence was too harsh and agree to allow an appeal for a lesser sentence. The defendant had been a model prisoner, and the judge ended up being an advocate.

Amazingly, the prosecutor in that case had received a serious promotion since agreeing to let this guy request a sentence reduction and was now the Attorney General.

As wonderful as it sounded, I was no model prisoner, and the prosecutor on my case always fought as if his or her face was still swollen from the brutal blows I landed during our fist fight in the alley of the courthouse. I knew I couldn't expect to be relieved of any time this way.

But the older brother was persistent, and he agreed to do all the research and type it at no cost! So a couple of weeks later, I once again had three irons in the fire. I still didn't feel like I had a chance, but at least, I remained active despite all my doubt.

So now with no classes to take, I just concentrated on avoiding trouble and waiting for the decision on all my motions, and the time was drawing near that I could be transferred back to a minimum security facility. I had not been tested in years, and I narrowly avoided a fight with my celly. He was a short-timer. They had given him two years for fraud, because he stole like $80,000 from several people. I shake my head at the thought that I got twenty-five years for about $8000 in drugs (according to the expert). So my celly wasn't entrenched in prison culture, and even though that was a good thing, it was going to be a problem for me.

He didn't see the problem with associating with child molesters and homosexuals. For this reason, we rarely spoke, and as long as he kept those associations away from the cell, I didn't need to act.

Well, it happened one day, there were about six of us involved in a good debate about the cost of jet fuel, and one of his molester buddies was a pilot allegedly, and he sought his opinion. As the debate died down and he and I were in the cell, the undesirable guy opened the door, gave his opinion on the matter, and didn't even show the proper respect by knocking or excusing himself as he entered.

The two of them then walked out together, but I followed quickly. One reason is because I was going to the library, and the second was so I could make sure he never ventured to my door again. I spoke harshly to both of them.

The molester tucked his tail and scurried along as he should. My celly took offense, which was good. Your manhood is important, but when he asked what I would do if he did not comply, I asked him to step into the cell, but he would not walk into that cell. He talked loud and made a scene, but he would not walk in that cell. Smart.

I left. He would have to go in the cell in a few hours for count, but during the two hours I was in the library, I cooled off, and when we went in the cell at count time, I saw him hesitate, but I put him at ease.

He still watched me closely for a couple of days, flinched if I moved too fast, smart, but there would be no more outward signs of conflict. I had too much to do. Besides, he would be released in the next couple of months.

In those couple of months, I used the altercation with him to introspect my motivation to survive the ordeal that is incarceration. At first, I just wanted to survive long enough to win an early release, but the later it got in my sentence, the less early any release would be, so I switched motivations to one of being more prepared to succeed than anyone anticipated.

But with it being painfully obvious that prison officials couldn't care less about prisoners' preparedness, my latest motivation was one that had always been present, just not adequately focused on. I had to survive prison without going crazy or "Brazy" as the guys from my car would say.

Enough time passed that I was officially put in for transfer back to a minimum security facility, and while I waited for the response and destination, I received word about my two-point reduction. Unsurprisingly, they would not be able to reduce my sentence due to the Statutory Mandatory Minimum I was sentenced under. No apologies, just disregard all the mail about a reduction, forget the 800 number, and get back to doing your time, this office will not be responding to any further inquiries on the matter.

That was the gist of one of the coldest Dear John letters I had ever received, and I had many to compare it to.

Chapter 10

Time to Breathe Thin Air

I was now up to about a dozen denials over the years, but I applaud the Public Defender's Office for The Department of Justice. They, too, are good at what they do, and all those who had relief coming received it. I watched guys with seventeen years get three years off and be eligible for transfers and drug classes they were otherwise unqualified for. I saw a guy with thirty years get a reduction to twenty-five years and complain because he was still left to serve one-and-a-half more years.

Once again, I was blessed to have a chance to go back to a minimum security place, maybe even close to home, and I used this knowledge to focus on the positive aspects of my own existence while the positive aspects of the guys around me seemed to make my positive shit just that, shit!

A month or so later, two in the morning, the officer beat on the cell door, flashed his light on my sleeping form, and said my name until I sat up and acknowledged that he was telling me it was time to transfer. I was told to put my belongings in mesh laundry bags, that it would be sorted and inspected at a later date and time by some un-named person, and all I needed to do was carry it to R&D and wait for my shackles and seat on the bus.

The six or seven hours it took on the straight drive to the transit center, I stayed awake, and reflected. I truly felt overwhelmed, but I was surrounded 24/7 by people I wish I'd never met so there wasn't much desire to confide in any of them, and thus my fears and troubles were mostly internalized. This was including the counselor who did not counsel, the Case Manager who solely wanted to manage my case and not me, and any psychologist on staff marginally interested in my problems at best, unless I became violent.

To the unavailable executive staff excluding the Captain whose answer to most questions or issues is a threat of placement in The Hole until someone else can get it figured out. Turns out I was finally going to the prison, or prison camp, that is thirty minutes from my last home. Blessed was indeed the word. I would need this reflection more than I realized!

Going back through transit with eighteen years under my belt was, in sorts, a pass, a driver's license that is good anywhere. More correctly, not being a snitch is and has always been my pass—however, in transit, being housed with guys who have life sentences and are headed from one Thunder Dome to another, with scars and stories to match their demeanor and outlooks on life, it isn't a badge of honor to be going to the prison camp. Those guys can't fathom a place with no fences, metal detectors, or serious gangs, so when it comes up in transit, and it will, I just focused on the time in. I served it well, and it shall do the same for me.

Sure enough, once at the transit center, I fell into my usual routine. I went to the assigned cell, met the celly, made my bed, searched for a cup, some hygiene items, and two books to read. Once I had these items, I did reconnaissance inside the unit. I went room to room, Spanish TV room, Sports TV room, and Movie room. I then found a perch or a fox hole and watched the guys move to see who had numbers, who the orderlies were, who appears too happy, scared, and who was worth talking to when a conversation must occur. Guys from all over the country, Texas, New York, Kansas, and other parts, a few in my car, but I would only reveal my membership when necessary because I could see some recklessness in these guys.

Two days into my four-day stay, it happened. I was doing dips in the upper common area, and one guy from Texas noticed I bothered to work out. Working out isn't just a sign of fitness, and it isn't just a way to expend energy or kill time—it shows a preparedness for physical confrontation. Each person has to decide if he wants to walk as a wolf or a sheep, or as my friend once said "as a Lion"! I always have to be between the Wolf and the Lion, however humbly as possible.

The guy from Texas asked where I was from, and for Blacks, this is not as basic as it sounds—he wasn't interested in knowing if I was from the Sunshine State, or the Hoosier State, or the Bicentennial State for purposes of planning a vacation sometime. In fact, he couldn't care less what state or city I was from unless the car, the group, the organization, the gang I was from interested him first. Not belonging makes you a sheep. Belonging makes you at least a Wolf, and you may be tested.

My standard answer "L form Denver, Black P Stone, my Neighborhood is called Park Hill" voice deeper, eyes low and focused, chest out, ears suddenly aware of all sounds. He smiled, told me that's what's up and introduced himself, and we embraced with a certain handshake. Then he asked that I forgive him for interrupting my workout. I told him no problem, and continued; he walked away. He was a talker, and his car was well-accounted for in this unit.

I shook my head wondering what would come of the introduction, but nothing really did, and I was glad of it. After all, I am a camper (minimal security) again now.

Another day goes by, and I see there is a little commotion at lunch. A youngster from Philly (he was in the car) had a bad habit of jumping the line, and a guy from Illinois called him on it. They were going to figure it out, and an invitation to the cell was sent. When I saw this, I found my perch—for security; mostly mine—but since the guy from Texas had done roll call and I was basically on count, I was in position to keep young Philly out of a jam if need be.

Once the issue was handled, a guy from New York wanted to confirm who I was. He understood I am from Denver Lanes in California—never allow such misinformation to get out about you. I repeated my standard, we embraced, and he had more questions: where I was going, how much time did I have. He was friendly, though, and he saw the way I moved during the incident. I told him I had almost eighteen years in with three to go.

He nodded his approval, and out of respect, I asked him where he was from. It turned out I did a couple of years with some guys he knows from the streets. With my credentials in order—and the mix-up about whether I was a Stone from the Junglez in California or the city of Denver now ironed out—I went back to my quiet existence for one more day, then I was out of there. Time to breathe thin air.

Chapter 11

A Period of Rebellion

The new place was small, real small, but small meant quiet, and that's what I wanted. Depending on halfway house, I could do as little as thirty months in this place or with my pending case and my petitions for clemency, I might leave as soon as I got there. No faith in that, but it was factual that the issues remained undecided.

I got acclimated quickly. As expected, I was in my home state, and people and things gravitated to me instantly, but as a rule, I don't like too many people. I won't ever forget all of these guys were people I wish I'd never met, and it took some real happenstance to make me see a person in prison as anything other than someone I met in prison. In twenty years, I have met five people I do and will keep in contact with. But I am seasoned, and I know how to conduct myself.

When you're new to a place, the secret is to act new and let all the characters introduce themselves to you, and in time, they will. Seek first to understand, then to be understood. I got a counselor I liked, a case manager I could not like because she could not like anyone else, and a few guys in awe of the amount of time I had been down. Then I recognized the guys who made it their business not to be in awe of the amount of time I had served. Once I got my job and started seeing my family and friends, time would fly!

Sure enough, and as always, my routine brought me into a zone, and the time was flying. I saw friends and family and got to discuss the legal issues I still had going. I was lifting weights, I was still keeping up my certification as a trainer, and I also found a decent set of DVDs on Spanish. The case manager was honest: this facility only cared that you worked. The only education they stressed was GED, so any other pursuits would be on me.

One night, I had a rather sad visitor—someone who used to be a fan was basically declaring their fandom over, and the visit was interrupted by an officer who had legal mail for me. This was highly unusual. I had to stop the visit and go sign for my legal mail. It was the decision on my motion to ask the prosecutor to admit I had too much time and that I wasn't that bad of a guy.

The prosecutor had refused this admission, but I did not get that notice first, I got the denial of the motion first, then the next day came the prosecutor's response. The prosecutor's office refused adamantly, it turns out. It didn't even hurt; that was just another thing I no longer had to worry about. Losing faith is hard to experience. Now down to one iron in the fire, my chances of being released early from the federal system were razor-thin.

This must have been the feeling the prosecutor wanted me to have: the deep despair, the agony of defeat, or at least the knowledge that defeat was inevitable. Would it have been better for me to feel hopeless and helpless sooner during my incarceration? Would it have served and suited the Justice Department better if I had been truly miserable this entire time?

The Federal Indictment says, "The United States of America v. E. L. Blackstone." I wonder if a poll of this entire nation would really support the sentence and the treatment throughout. If the lady from Idaho and the man from New Hampshire are 100% behind the twenty-five-year investment that has been made in me.

How lucky I was. My sentencing range was ten years to life, with the statute sitting inside of it saying that twenty-five years is the minimum I could receive, basically making my sentencing range twenty-five years to life. Sounds like a murderer's sentence, except murderers aren't sentenced so harshly half of the time. I recall vividly my attorney's frustration when he tried to explain to me that we could not win. Undoubtedly, he thought I was stupid or delusional, but the source of his frustration was not my stupidity or lack of understanding his message.

The Pledge of Allegiance says "One Nation Under God" and I had faith in that. It didn't seem crazy or naive. I believe in order to accomplish something, you must have faith in the endeavor. My attorney was frustrated by my ignorance—he was frustrated, but he left me ignorant. If he would have told me one fact about a Federal Criminal Trial, I would have tapped out, begged for mercy, and saved myself at least ten years. He did not tell me the jury would be required to determine my guilt without knowing my punishment. Did you know it was like that for federal criminal juries?

Perhaps I assumed all trials were like those on television shows or on the news. If a murderer gets a sentence of twenty-five to life, what sort of sentence would a juror, in a drug case with no violence, suspect might be levied?

I didn't find out the jury wouldn't know I was facing twenty-five to life until it was too late. I actually thought it was a slam dunk acquittal because everyone would convict me based on the evidence and sentence me to twenty-five-year at minimum for drugs and a gun. The jury would convict, and contrary to what the judge said, he would not determine the punishment—the AUSA had already decided that.

I had faith in humanity, but humanity had been removed from the equation. The only discretion was that of the prosecutor, and everyone knows there is no mercy in a pit-bull. In fact, the only way to stop a pit-bull from killing their foe is by killing the dog. Career-wise, prosecutors can't be killed—they can't be tamed or trained. They keep killing lives, spirits, hopes, and dreams sanctioned by Congress and One Nation Under God.

It took a while for me to notice it, but each time I was denied a chance at early release, there would be a period of rebellion for me. It's as juvenile as it sounds, but it's true. I look back, and I have decided it is in my most basic nature to respond, react, re-coil on some level when I am denied or rejected, and I suppose it is human nature.

So along with making plans to get my driver's license (I told you I liked the counselor), making another attempt to be bi-lingual, securing a good prison job, maintaining my fitness certifications, maintaining my fitness, and enjoying my visits with family and friends, I started taking liberties again, once again failing to see how lucky I was in that instant and abusing the freedoms I was afforded. It is next to impossible to respect those who don't respect you, and although most jailers are not hard liners and are usually there just for the paycheck, they represented the evil empire that had been so harsh in their continued torturous cycles of implied sentence relief followed by complete refusal to grant it.

I had been contrite about a decade and a half ago. I was sorry for things I had done that had never come to light. I was regretful of decisions I made that led to my prison sentence, and I vowed to never come close to the legal line ever again let alone cross it. We teach our children that sincere contrition leads to forgiveness, and I was sure at one point, I was a child, a product of my environment, and just as I had found trouble, there would be some smart and kind people who would share the sentencing judge's early assessment that twenty-five years in prison was a waste of my potential.

But now after more than twenty years, with my potential wasted, who is going to be allowed to cry over the spilled milk that has been my life? I don't get to cry because I was legally and lawfully convicted by a jury of my peers. The citizens of the US don't get to cry because, according to the document, they were all in on it. The government can't cry because they were the sole investors in my punishment.

So just as we all had to have faith in the process that brought me here, we all must have faith in the product this process produces.

I had to lie, sneak, and cheat my way into the majority of the classes I took so the lesson on honesty may have missed the mark. I spent most of my time in prison away from my home state so the ideal of family ties has not been adequately encouraged. I worked my way down from High Security to Minimum Security through good behavior, and this accomplishment, while rewarding, doesn't establish the systemic relief that people in my position are truly working for. I had not been rehabilitated—not by the programs and incentives of the BOP, I can tell you this for sure. I had been punished, and at that point, I was seeking revenge, not redemption.

I felt this way as I sat in the relatively cozy confines of a cubicle at a prison camp. I had a microwave, I watched cable TV, I ate pretty good meals, I was not told how or where to move under the watchful eye of a zealous officer all day. I was not required to carry protection from violence. There were rarely any fights where I was, but I felt this way still: I wanted those who took part in my suffering to suffer.

I had not forgiven those who would not forgive me. But I was a minimum security prisoner, non-violent, and almost home with this chip on my shoulder. Imagine if you will the guy who was forced to do his entire twenty-five years behind a fence, with the killers, rapists, overt racists, and had to protect himself every waking moment from the violence that goes with being in a place where some people won't leave the prison, ever.

About 85% of people in prison will be released. What if they all feel as I did? Has the investment in our misery been worth the possible return? I'm not talking anarchy, or any kind of revolution, but so many people have been locked up for so long, you cannot avoid ex-convicts in public any more. We have seen horrors you can't and don't want to imagine.

We are at your mercy for employment and health care, and a second chance at a normal life, but after being caged for twenty-five years, how can I be normal—how can we be normal? All that time invested in what, a punishment whose intent was realized a decade and a half ago?

Chapter 12

As Slow As a Sloth

I kept working on my plans, I kept doing my time, I kept consciously and purposely disregarding the rules, and as much as I felt like I had to look forward to, I was mostly living in the moment and trying not to let the moment conquer me.

I was looking forward to starting a business when I got out, and I had planned extensively for the idea. I was planning to relocate from my home state, and along with my positive influence, I had researched, discussed, and debated that idea, but I was forced by my reality to stay in the moment. It just seemed like those moments should have ended, passed, or concluded, and the cruel aspect of unusual *and* cruel punishment simply wouldn't let me leave them behind.

Believe it or not, though, my work ethic and my belief that my personal standards will be my saving grace still applied. I performed my duties beyond satisfaction in most cases, and I was reminded of this by the new counselor who placed his trust in me while he was getting acclimated to being a counselor, and I never let him down. Through his eyes, I was seen by the new Camp Administrator, and I was eventually offered a chance to have a job that would allow me to leave the facility every weekday, drive to a city not far from where I grew up, and interact with people not directly involved with my incarceration.

But because of the liberties I had taken at the last minimum security place, I was given a probation period. This made the offer not so attractive, but I did not decline. I continued to work and be as effective as ever, but I was skeptical about the probationary period and if they would actually give me the assignment.

My skepticism wasn't just my overall negative attitude about the BOP from my past experience, it was because there was a guy they had working who desperately wanted to not have that job and would sometimes sabotage the crew. They would not replace him with me until we were both tormented by the process. Common sense isn't so common. If two people apply for a job as a cook and one of those people loves to cook while the other just needs a job—who would you hire?

So while I kept up my appearances and my work never suffered, I kept up my shenanigans, as well. I would not deprive myself in hope of receiving rewards from the captors or oppressors.

Things were kind of good, though. Those visits, meeting two of my grandsons, seeing my nieces and nephews, meeting the great-nieces and nephews, looking at my last surviving sibling when she could visit, it was all chicken soup. We even were lucky enough to have an officer in the visiting room who wasn't interested in making visits awkward and unpleasant.

Yeah, by prison standards, things were okay. Until...

The current President's term was coming to an end, and his clemency project would be, too.

They contacted us and told us that all petitions would be answered in the beginning. There had been five guys at this prison camp who had already received clemency, and I had not been denied, so I held out a modicum of hope that I would read my name in the last round of clemency.

When the list was released, it was huge; I think it was over a thousand names. I saw guys' names I knew from early in my prison sentence, but I did not see mine. Then the email came from my clemency project lawyer. I was denied on the last day.

Glass half-full or half-empty? Did I survive until the last cut like a ball player almost good enough for the team, or had my petition been tossed to the side long ago with the denial pending all the while?

But I was lucky to be at a minimum security facility to finish my complete sentence. Really! I had my family close, and I could draw off their energy until I was able to absorb the hit. I had a cellmate who suffered the same fate as me. We didn't discuss it—there was no need to discuss what was already understood. He also would begin taking liberties since the incentive had been removed from him, as well, another thing that was innately understood.

I also had some love coming from across the country. And for me to feel so broken by a decision I had no real faith in, I needed all the love I could get, and I was made to feel special during a real bad time.

Now with no more remedies or plans of action for an early release, all I could do was play the hand I was dealt. Enjoy myself as much as my morals would allow. Perform my duties as a prisoner and try to earn a social furlough, and some extra halfway house. Time to break up the monotony and depressing state of just being in prison. I had my routine. Routine gets you by in prison—routine is synonymous with being institutionalized in many ways.

Waking up early to walk or to exercise before breakfast doesn't seem to be a dangerous thing. It sounds as positive and productive as it is, until it isn't. When for some reason, you aren't able—or more correctly, you aren't allowed your morning walk or you can't go to the gym for exercise—your day is thrown off, and you never recover. Your time alone to pray or meditate has been canceled, and your ability to adjust all your gauges for yet another day in a personal hell has been taken away.

Your outlet, your method of removing stress or built-up frustration or anger through weights or other activity, has been blocked. Some would say it's the same in the free world, but it isn't. I cannot say enough how in prison, you are surrounded by people all day every day that you wish you'd never met. There is no escaping the eventual resentment you feel for them and they feel for you, and in order for there to be peace in the most tame of prisons, the guys who vent physically must be allowed to do so.

Plus the routines are so tightly regimented, if you bench press on Tuesday at 7:45 a.m. and you finish at 8:30, it isn't because that is the perfect time for you—it's because someone else was bench pressing from 7:00 a.m. until 7:45, and someone else will be in at 8:30 and they have their own problems and agendas. They don't give a damn about your routine being thrown off. They need to take care of themselves. You can't be late, early, run over, or deviate too far without proper notice, and even with that, it had better not clash with what has already been established as routine.

I would sit in one chair in one spot every day. My chair. My spot. If challenged or questioned, I'd explain it's the routine that has worked with the other established guys. Not affected by routine are new guys who are constantly seeking routine, and guys about to be released who are no longer held together by the cords of their routine in prison.

After breakfast, I would go about my duties of working, cleaning my cell, exercising, showering, having lunch, then returning to work, exercising again after work, showering again, preparing for count, then eating dinner, studying and/or watching TV. This was my routine six days a week, with only small variations from time to time. Not only do you use routine to map out the day and pass time, because we don't really do much compared to free people, the time moves slower for us, and we fill our days with a small laundry list of things to do, and there are times and places it gets worse, like in transit or in The Hole.

In The Hole, you are fed three times a day, and the only other activities are showers which are a huge deal because they are only every other day. Going to recreation which is a dog kennel and then there is the mail call. Visits from staff or a new person put in The Hole become entertainment for the entire tier, and the conversation about the special event lasts until the night comes.

In The Hole, you slow your existence down in a way that is comparable to the way a sloth has a slow metabolism. A sloth moves so slowly that falling out of a tree can take all day, and that is how you must handle activities in The Hole. You have to allow eating, showering, and a letter to take up your whole day.

After a while, showering will hold the same physiological properties as a good weight-lifting session, and this is a good thing. How else do you cope or survive being in such segregated quarters? What takes talent and patience is describing or explaining such a sad and boring fruitless existence to a loved one who doesn't understand that there is nothing to talk about. Most days in prison are literally like spending the day in a prison.

Some people in prison give up on trying to communicate all nuances of the place. Then family ties suffer, and the concerned loved one can't imagine how not calling them or using them to vent is better than picking up the phone or in more recent years sending an email, but you strive to keep your friends and family as part of your routine. You have the awkward calls, the letters with no content, the visits with no excitement, and you pray that everyone involved is able to keep it up for your entire three, five, ten, twelve, and in my case, twenty-five-year sentence.

Then my routine was broken like a motherfucker!

I was summoned to the office of the Captain and SIS Lieutenant, and that was never good. It is the equivalent of having a police officer's card left on your front door. If you don't have an idea of why they were at your house, they could have been there for anything except something good.

Chapter 13

Fighting With the Monster

There was an investigation. I thought they were aware of all my liberties and disrespect of their rules, but they weren't. Not specifically, but they knew one of their staff didn't care about prisoners taking liberties, and they decided they would get rid of him.

I worked for him in one of my job assignments so the SIS Officers thought I would be key in stopping him from allowing said liberties. Ironic because there is never a time when a prisoner's word is taken over an officer's, so when they told me to tell everything the officer was allowing the prison population to get away with or face being shipped across the country away from my family and back behind a fence, I had three things I needed to convey.

1) If I was into snitching, I wouldn't have been on year twenty of my prison sentence.

2) No prisoner's word can convict an officer, in a room full of officers.

And 3) I didn't want to transfer, but I could finish my time anywhere.

I spent the entire summer in The Hole, and one morning, they woke me up to pack my belongings. I was being transferred the next day. With no sanction or conviction, back in cuffs and shackles.

In a couple of ways, the transfer was better than sitting in The Hole hoping to be returned to that compound. For one, as I sat in The Hole under what was called an "investigation," I wasn't allowed contact by phone, visit, or email with any of my loved ones for the first two weeks of the eight-week ordeal. I wasn't even allowed contact with staff. Yep, my counselor and case manager couldn't even contact me. The second reason had to deal with the case manager directly.

After serving so much time, I was finally coming into the part of my sentence where we could dare talk about releasing back into society, and my halfway house placement would be the subject and highlight of my latest six-month review.

But after serving twenty years, this case manager felt like I needed to be able to explain in vivid detail why I should be granted the maximum allowable time in the halfway house. Which I could explain in my sleep...

However, her discretion was the hurdle, and I know just like I know my name that no amount of sensible explanation or reasoning would convince this person to recommend more than six months halfway house—which is not really a release from prison, more of a work release with perks.

So I tried to believe it was a sign that I was transferred so quickly. That's right, eight weeks was fast. I had expected to be in The Hole six months. A sign I may be able to get more halfway house and a better start from another case manager in another prison.

So there I was in the desert at a new, quiet facility, waiting for some good news. When I first encountered the new case manager, I immediately liked his style. He seemed no nonsense, but easy-going. He paid attention to my paperwork. He saw that my projected release date coincided with the timeline for submitting halfway house paperwork. This actually should have been done while I was in The Hole, but it wasn't, and I might just benefit from the neglect. He asked if I had already done my halfway house request, and I told him no, then the man winked at me.

Just like that, the music stopped.

Complete silence for ten seconds while I tried to figure out what he would say next, because the wink was something I was totally unprepared for, for too many reasons to try to make sense of. Then he looked at my puzzled expression and proceeded to tell me that as a case manager, he was of a rare breed, that he would try to give me what I had coming.

The light came on at that statement. My new case manager whose name I either did not know yet or did not remember when he said it had in our first minute of contact offered me more hope than every other officer I had ever encountered in the BOP. Not including the one Black officer in Minnesota who used to put up on a bulletin board trivia and current event questions and offer rewards for the correct answers. Often, the questions dealt with realities of life after prison.

Then, he said his name or he repeated it, and I would remember it surely from now on. He told me to see him the following Wednesday, and we would get the ball rolling.

To leave the prison six months sooner than I expected would be an excellent tradeoff for the inconvenience of my family and friends because, in the end, me being able to work on my redemption six months sooner was a greater joy than sharing sodas and chips while we talk about what a joy it would be when we no longer had to visit in a monitored setting.

This place was smaller than the last place. It had fewer people, no more than twenty Blacks. It is no coincidence or accident that Blacks are held in minimum security prisons at a lesser rate than all the other races according to my experience, but the reasons are far too complex and evil for me to try to shed the proper light on, in my modest little book.

This place had no weights, no recreational setups common in prisons, no pool tables, no handball courts, and no restroom facilities on the outer yard. So it was as boring as it sounds when I tell you it sits in a desert. The housing area was literally a warehouse. The concrete floors still had tape on them marking boundaries for storage of pallets and machinery, with the pipes and tubing exposed on the ceiling above me as I wrote. There is a sticker with an arrow indicating the direction of the flow of the domestic cold water.

The other building was nice, though. It had a couple of class rooms or multi-purpose rooms, the medical department was fully functional, the visiting area was nice, and the dining situation was five star by BOP standards.

I had come with the notion of having fourteen months left to serve before I would go to the halfway house, but with the possibility of only having to be here for eight months, I was looking at this place through rose-colored glasses. I hurried to get acclimated, discovering that the Black guys who had seniority over the Black IVs were more Lifetime and SYFY movies guys than football and basketball, which told me to immerse myself in the books.

I didn't have enough time to make them understand me, and this was actually better for all parties involved. I enrolled in a couple of classes, not to impress the staff because I no longer did things in prison to please or appease them, but to fill my days with academic efforts.

So while I waited for my halfway house date, I took the opportunity to write this condensed account of my journey through the Federal Prison System. With no way of knowing if the rumors of a change in policy or budget cuts to the halfway house system were true, with no way of knowing if my case manager was who he said he was, or if he was in disguise from the moment we met. With no way of knowing if I will finish my sentence without a single lucky break or good fortune until the halfway house date is returned and then I am released with no more than a-hundred-and-eighty days to prepare for my future after more than seven-thousand-and-three-hundred days of paying for my past—I am fighting with the monster that has grown inside of me for all these years.

Chapter 14

The Difference Between a Traitor and a Hero

Fifteen years ago, I was ready to spend my life making up for what I did in my community. Showing, teaching, leading any who would listen to my life's lessons...

But the last fifteen years have knocked that desire, that need, out of me. I don't expect good things from many people now. Being in prison has shown me the worst part of everyone I knew before I was thrown in the trash and locked away and everyone I have met since I've been inside the belly of the beast. It has shown me the effectiveness and success of ruthlessness; how complete and total domination can be sustained and used to promote and preserve an evil and selfish interest.

I have learned in the school of hard knocks in the University of the Penitentiary that mercy is not an option. I understand that you do indeed kill ants with a hammer. I now know you should overdo all deeds necessary to win rather than half-ass them. I see there is no place for someone willing to seem weak. I have witnessed the system, when unsure of itself, eliminate its captive and use the act of purging as a platform to collect more votes, money, land, and assets to do more of the same, in an effort to correct or fix what can't be fixed.

How can a sane product be created by a manufacturer of insanity?

It took them a long time to turn me into a beast of worthy reflection. It takes constant effort and pressure and darkness to create the monster within. Now I may be instructed to pick up the pieces in a-hundred-and-eighty days as if I had only been gone for that amount of time.

It is up to me to want it, to strive for it, to make it happen, all with the caveat that they better like the way I go about it, or else, they'll put me back in the cage.

The irony is how I am now more comfortable inside that cage. The cage I tried so desperately to avoid, the cage the people of the United States of America built and maintained at a cost of $30,000 a year for twenty-one years and two months for me. The government invested over $600,000 in me. What sort of return do they really expect on their investment?

When I was growing up, I remember idolizing anyone who seemed popular. My favorite neighbors were the ones who threw the parties or had lots of company. As a child, the activity was so exciting. My favorite cousins were the ones who had lots of friends—the ones who seemed happy, they could do wheelies on their bikes, they could dance and dress well. Those who were always entertaining and the sources of smiles and laughter.

My favorite friends were the kids who had the toys and the free time and space to just go all out all the time. We could play and be kids and not have a sense of time or care about life or its challenges.

As I grew and got farther away from our front porch, as I ventured off our block, as I saw the avenues and boulevards that bordered our neighborhood, I was able to see and experience more impressive things than just my friends and family while they were at ease.

When you're a kid and you're allowed to walk to the corner store on your own for the first time, life changes—opens up. When you go to the corner store with no adult escort, you get to move slowly, be nosey, stare at people and things, focus on what catches your eye and not hurry along at the command of your escort. People allow you to see them in ways they don't reveal in front of adult chaperones. You'll hear kids cursing or discussing subject matter beyond their maturity levels. Adults with lesser morals will engage in acts they, too, keep hidden from responsible adults.

At the corner stores, there are so many characters, a young kid could just sit and watch and be more entertained by than watching any TV show. In minority communities, the corner store is either also the liquor store or is close to the liquor store, and as fascinating as the general store is, it is a convalescence home compared to the liquor store. Whoa, the characters are enhanced, the traffic is doubled and faster, and being able to experience the sights of these businesses without a filter was always inviting to me.

I would volunteer to go to the store for the iffiest of runs. I could run, racing dogs or my shadow down the sidewalks on my way, or I could take my bike racing other bikes whether they knew we were racing or not, and of course racing the cars on the side streets to the stop sign which were the equalizers. But whatever my mode or method, I always wanted to get to the store, always some action.

Now, when I tell you I was drawn to popular people, I want you to know that as far as I was concerned, the clerks at the various stores in the small shopping center and stand-alone stores were rock stars to me. They knew everybody, they knew everything about the store, they could make or break your purchase, and they always seemed to have something going outside the store, not really involving the store but made possible because of the store.

And as star-struck as I would be by them, it was almost inconceivable to me how humbled the clerks would be when the actual owners of the store would make an appearance. When the person whose name was on the sign was in the house, there was a noticeable change in everyone, not celebrity, but royalty in my young eyes. The owners captivated those who captivated me, and it was confusing to see. Confusing but alluring.

At a very young age, I knew I wanted to work as a clerk so I could be cool and popular and in demand as those I watched go about their business without a clue as to the affect they had on me. And when I was older, I would own a store, and maybe even a liquor store. The word was too big for me then, but I wanted to be an entrepreneur.

Over the years, I would learn more about these stores, the characters, and the nuances, not all flattering but none so discouraging that I would abandon my dream to one day have a business of my own. The older I got, the more I learned; the more I learned, the more I wanted to know, and the more I knew, the more I was sure that wines, spirits, liquor, and vice were products that are timeless, bulletproof, and recession-proof.

I mean, think about it: bars, clubs, and restaurants are expensive, and they require a commitment to something other than the vice. But the liquor store has no such demands on your time. All you have to do is be in line while the store is open and have ID that says you're twenty-one or older. With much lower standards and easy membership, no wonder the parking lot stays full. No tips required. The only talk is talk that you initiate.

The owner and workers at a liquor store are always popular—their goods and services always in demand. People who have a bad experience at a liquor store will return with money in hand. The liquor store, or "LQ" as I was taught to call it, has everything you could want or need once you satisfy the original purpose for entering one. Alcohol, cigarettes, snacks, condoms, and even an illicit market that thrives on the fringes of all LQs—people who will buy for underage drinkers, people who will hang out by the store for reasons that range from it being a place to find like-minded drinkers to staying close so they are not too far away from it when it is closing time for that last purchase, to those who use the traffic and seedy nature of some LQs to sustain other markets for vice.

Romantic situations are fostered at LQs. The relationship between a person and their LQ persons is as real and vital as any with a barber, bartender, bus driver, or banker. People love the LQ and rush to take their money inside and leave out with the liquid-filled containers and cigarettes, and snacks, and condoms!

Growing up, I learned people are lifelong slaves to what the LQ sells, but no one called it that ever. It was legal, still is legal, and it is so important and accepted that the Constitution was changed to preserve the right to buy and sell alcohol.

How could an aspiring young entrepreneur not be interested in a liquor store as a business? Well, if you have ever looked into the industry, you know it takes way more than a simple notion and a sales tax license. So much more that to own a liquor store is out of the realm of possibility for most. But my eyes never turned blind to the economics of the business, the vice, the opportunity.

Don't think I was hatched as a future drug dealer. Don't think that as soon as I was able to be out of my parents' sight, I yearned to peddle drugs, and that I'm using the example of the legal drug alcohol as an excuse. I grew up hating the effects of drugs and alcohol in my family, my home, never mind the community. What ended up being stronger than that hate was my fondness for the money that could be had from people's loyalty to those products. Pardon me if I sound like a cigarette company, but it is true. So many legal drugs to sell, and there was no way into the game.

So I scratched my entrepreneurial itch via a janitorial company. Steady work, but not the same demand. People accept the janitor, but they don't cherish him or his service like they do a store owner and her goods.

Next up, I tried to open a record store. People got to have music, but I was too small. My sister and my parents had my back—we even had the backing of a friend of the family who was a local DJ. It was novelty, not success with financial gain. I would look out the window as I played music for the shopping center our store was in. Cars would zoom by, and people on foot would scurry by all headed to the LQ down the block. Sometimes, once the spirits were obtained, they would come in and buy music for the evening's events, but most of the customers in the center were there because of the LQ or at least they would have some connection to some vice in close proximity.

Please understand that I don't see it as a negative. I didn't have a personal ill will to the LQ or the other outside stores for other vice. I know of the urgent need for the items at the LQ. I learned of it from my family. Without judging their sickness or vulnerability, I simply wanted my cash register to ring like the one at the LQ. When kids younger than I—and I was seventeen—started coming to the record store with more cash in their pockets than I had in the cash register, I took notice. They dealt in vice.

Eventually, so would I. I would be loved and revered, and my arrival would be anticipated. I would stop having the telephone service cut off at my parents' house. We would always have food and gas money. I learned about patience and struggle and honesty and integrity from my wonderful parents, who happened to collectively be hooked on every legal drug sold over the counter at a retail store. I entered into the drug business out of necessity, but I wanted to be a local celebrity; I wanted to give jobs, open stores, be a pillar of the community.

I would have gone to college if it would have been economically feasible. With my mission and goals in the front of my mind, I sold drugs with a clear conscience. I was fair, respectful, prompt, and provided quality goods and services, just like any person who did business and wanted to succeed. I wasn't twisted or evil, I didn't see myself as killing my community. I was certainly no worse than the LQ who sold alcohol to men with liver disease and who stumbled in their stores already drunk as if they could actually get drunker.

I was no worse than the corner store who sold cigarettes to the skinny lady with the terrible cough who was diagnosed with lung cancer but cannot stop smoking because the pain of withdrawal is worse than the disease that is killing her while the whole world watches. I never sold anything to someone who wasn't an adult, or who didn't want it, and I knew that if they didn't get it from me, they would go to someone else. Just like a person who couldn't find their brand of liquor, cigarettes, or coffee at one store simply goes to another.

I discovered vice was the way, or at least I thought it was —so smart I was stupid. But this clear conscience and free will stayed with me my entire life, and I have spent almost half of my life in prison on this one case. And because I molded my behavior after staples of our community and the people who operated them, I always felt like the law had a double standard and I was tasked with overcoming the unfair laws and poverty.

As I write this, my home state now allows marijuana sales, retail stores that sell vice. There are people locked away for that exact crime, and I am locked away for a similar crime. Turns out my eye wasn't completely off. I wasn't just some youngster who wanted to make easy money. There are entire states who agree that vice is profitable and doable. I heard a quote in a movie—it said that the difference between a traitor and a hero was timing, or the outcome of the war.

Has life shown me I was ahead of my time? Or that I was captured in the war but my side eventually won, or at least won enough battles for there to still be a war? When I am released, how should I feel about the Pot Stores that now outnumber the LQs in my state? Of the $600,000 that was invested in my punishment, 1/20th could have been invested in my store, my establishment of vice, and I, too, would have been a tax-paying businessman in my neighborhood.

Chapter 15

My Indentured Servitude

How can I return to a society that punished me so unequivocally, so unforgivingly, but now, they reward some other hustler just like me? I feel like the investment expenditures were really uneven. I just sit here now with days until my release.

When you're under a year, you can call it what you want—months, weeks, or days. I have to take serious inventory. I have multiple feelings about my experience at all times. From one moment to the next, I can go from hopeful and positive and looking forward to the future...to depressed and sullen about all the time I have been locked away...to angry about my past and eager to exact my revenge on my future.

It is said that if prison doesn't change you, you were already fucked up when you got there. But it cuts both ways: incarceration may correct some criminals, but I know for a fact that it creates them.

After twenty years, I have been able to relive my arrest, my method, and my outcomes so many times. All I am sure of is how I would do it differently if I did it again. I can't tell you if I would commit another crime, but I can tell you I am not afraid of prison anymore.

I don't know if I'll be a good worker once I'm released. I don't know if my plans to be a business owner will come to fruition, but I do know that I am used to being housed, fed, and cared for, and if I was put back in this situation again, I know I would survive.

I don't know if fresh air, freedom to come and go as I please, and the ability to choose my course of action will remove the bitterness buried deep inside me, but I do know I hate all who were a part of my indentured servitude.

I have tried not to go crazy. I have tried to maintain my sanity.

I have been blessed to have love and support, even as I suffered so severely during this prison time. But I won't know if I'm sane until it's over, until my life is over and my actions post-prison indicate that over seven-thousand-and-three-hundred days behind bars didn't ruin me for the rest of my days.

My impending exit is a warning to anyone who has ever invested in anything. To expect to get out what you put in is so basic, it's comical to expect for me to do anything but fail once I am released. To the people of the United States of America as they were when versus E. L. Blackstone and they are now. After having forgotten about the $30,000 a year, and moving on to more current issues while I was forced to live each day painfully reminded of the past long after the point had faded.

There is an army of people just like me entering society gradually, steadily. Pay attention to your investment. How else can you realize your return?

God Bless America, I pray for us all.

Acknowledgments

You know who you are. Claim it, own it—I cannot tell your story for you.

About the Author

E. L. Blackstone is an author, federal prison strategist and consultant who draws from 21 years of firsthand experience inside the federal prison system. He works with individuals preparing for federal custody, providing practical insight into institutional culture, unwritten dynamics and how to navigate incarceration with greater awareness and intention.

Work with E. L. Blackstone

FEDERAL PRISON CONSULTING

There are aspects of entering federal custody that a sentencing hearing, handbook or legal briefing cannot fully prepare you for.

Drawing from 21 years of firsthand experience, E. L. Blackstone provides private consulting for individuals and families preparing for federal incarceration and those currently navigating the federal prison system.

Consulting focuses on understanding the environment, institutional culture and unwritten dynamics; preparing mentally and practically for incarceration, using time intentionally and planning for what comes next.

Email: Roiconsultant@icloud.com

Consulting services do not constitute legal representation or legal advice.

www.ingramcontent.com/pod-product-compliance
Lightning Source LLC
LaVergne TN
LVHW051932051126
851857LV00020B/2077
9798997516802